For Joan, Cordelia, Suria & Honor.
For Ezra & Little Felix.
To Ann and Family.
To Tiger Alf and for Luis & Family.

Contents

THE DAY MY LITTLE BROTHER TURNED INTO A DINOSAUR

for Ezra and Felix.

What can I say?
It was a great day
He suddenly started to roar
He grew a claw,
1, 2, 3 then 4!
His bottom turned into a tail
His skin became like the shell of a snail.
Then he started biting the sofa
Then he ate the toaster!
Next he went on a rampage,
Dad said let's put him in a cage
Grandadda said let's put him on stage –
And charge money,
Everyone will find a dinosaur little brother funny!
But mum said let's put him to bed,
Sleep will get that dinosaur out of his head.
And sure enough the next morning
He had stopped roaring.
He was once again a little brother,
Just like any other,
Because sleep will never fail,
Except he still had his dinosaur tail!

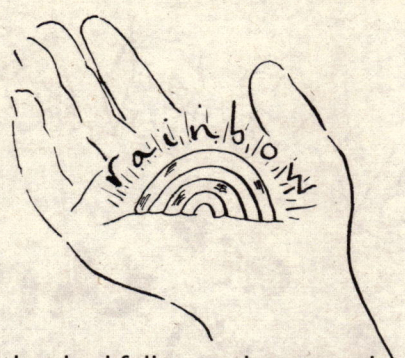

I rescued a rainbow that had fallen to the ground.
It was lost and looking to be found.
It was a baby rainbow
And didn't know which way to go.
I told it that on Earth,
You and your kind are famous,
You were the sign that said the NHS has come to save us.
We sing songs about you,
How your colours are so perfect and true.
We even wear rainbow shoe laces and badges,
That show anyone can be special friends with anyone,
Because life is all about different kinds of matches.
The baby rainbow blushed
And seemed quite chuffed.
But then it started to cry
And said,
'That's great to hear,
But how do I get back in the sky?'
I told the baby rainbow,
'That's not where you need to be,
You see you are just a sticker,
That's fallen off some kids coat.
But wherever you are,
The sky, the ground or on a child,
You always give us hope.'

BABIES are funny things

They make me laugh in every different way,
All those funny things they try to say.
They eat your fingertips
And wooden building bricks.
They start to laugh if you just hide your face
Then they throw things all over the place.
They copy what you do,
They like their meals to look like goo.
They wake you up in the middle of the night
As soon as they get teeth, they will give you a bite.
They're happy in nappy.
All they ever say is more or mum, they stare at everyone,
They also lick the floor with their tongue.
When they start to toddle they waddle,
Like ducks they head for the nearest puddle.
They are mostly bald like potatoes,
But some have so much hair
A bird could have a nest in there.
Babies can be magical little things.
They'd be even cuter
If they had wings.

THE BADGER WHO CAME FOR BREAKFAST

inspired by
the
wonderful
Judith Kerr

It happened one morning
Without any warning,
A badger walked in
And sat down with a grin.
Nothing was discussed
But it wanted breakfast.
So, we gave it eggs on toast –
It liked the eggs the most!
We said, 'Would you like orange juice, coffee or tea?'
The badger replied, 'All three.'
We mixed it together and served it in a plant-pot,
The badger drank the lot.
The badger said breakfast is fun
And asked for another one.
This time we gave it porridge –
The badger liked this,
Saying, 'It's better than having to forage in the forest.'
We said, 'Would you like a hash brown?'
But the badger said it didn't have time –
It had to meet a friend in town.
We asked who it was going to see.
The badger replied,
'My friend the tiger, we are meeting up for tea!'

Waiting for today, waiting for tomorrow,
Waiting to lend and waiting to borrow.
Waiting for the rush, waiting for the hush,
Waiting for the bus
And waiting for the rest of us.
Waiting for the beginning,
Waiting to see who ends up winning.
Waiting for the Sellotape,
Waiting for the cake,
Waiting for a chance to escape,
Waiting for the next piece of chocolate!
Waiting to send.
Waiting on a friend,
Will waiting never end?

In the Halloween highway code,
Broom parking only, all others will be toad!
Zombies ahead,
Always give way to the living dead.
Dracula is arriving...
What's he driving – a van-pire! That's got a fang flat tyre!
Ghosts on the road!
Keep the car windows closed.
Headless horsemen at night,
Not only do they not have a head,
They've also not got a headlight!
Skeleton crossing
Watch out for skulls going shopping.
Pirate lane only,
Only to be used by those with a black flag that's boney.
Haunted roundabout,
Give way to Egyptian Mummies walking about.
Spooky service station,
You might meet the Adams family on vacation.
But it's got a *Corpsta*-Coffee
That's always dead frothy.

Scooby Doo
And the rest of the mystery solving crew,
Could have saved themselves a lot of time and trouble,
If they just went down to the mask and costume hire shop
A bit more frequently...
And asked, 'Who's bought what recently?'

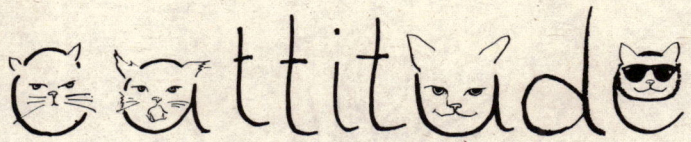

cattitude

Cats have got cattitude!
They walk about with a funny look on their face.
They walk about as if they own the place.
They think everywhere is their own personal space.
They lick their fur as if it's good to taste,
Cos' cats have got cattitude!
They are always having a cat nap.
They purr sweetly, then suddenly attack.
They expect a little cat snack
And when they don't get one they turn their back.
Cos' cats have got cattitude!
They think you are their servant
They think nothing is urgent.
They think they're a secret agent.
Weirdest of all,
They poke their noses in each others bottoms with
amazement!
Now if we did that it would just be rude,
But cats can get away with it
Because they have got cattitude!

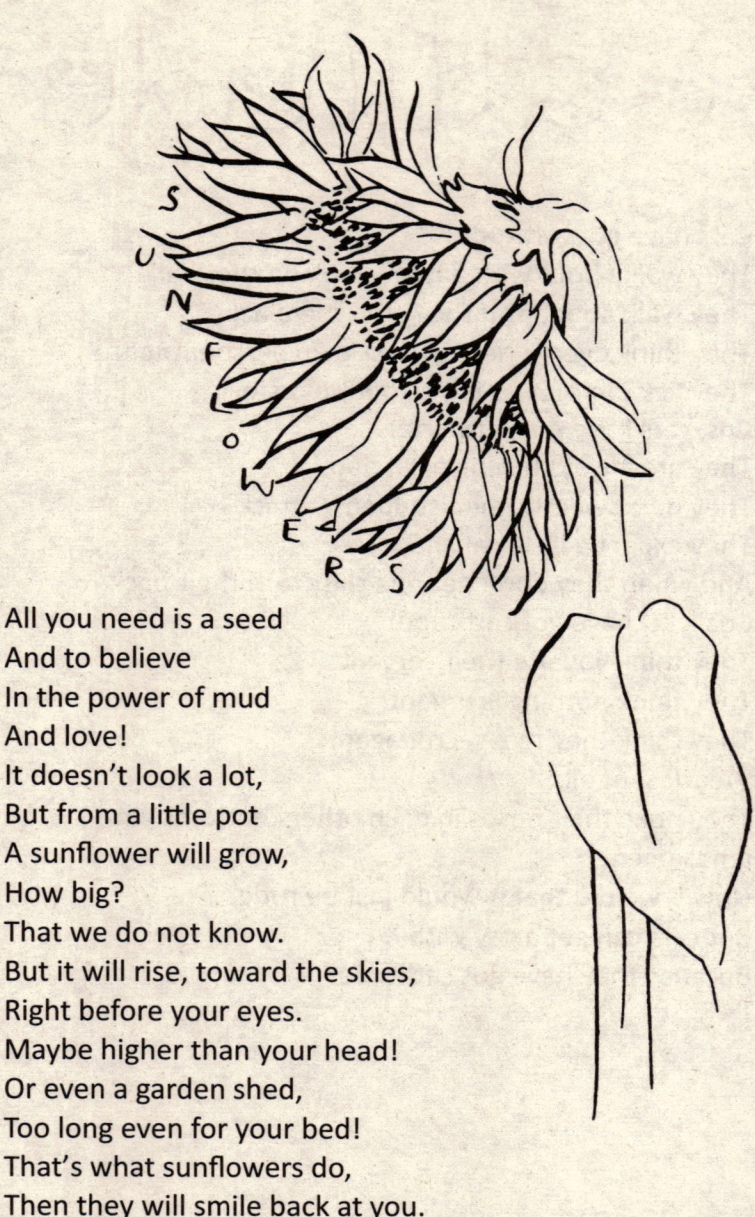

All you need is a seed
And to believe
In the power of mud
And love!
It doesn't look a lot,
But from a little pot
A sunflower will grow,
How big?
That we do not know.
But it will rise, toward the skies,
Right before your eyes.
Maybe higher than your head!
Or even a garden shed,
Too long even for your bed!
That's what sunflowers do,
Then they will smile back at you.

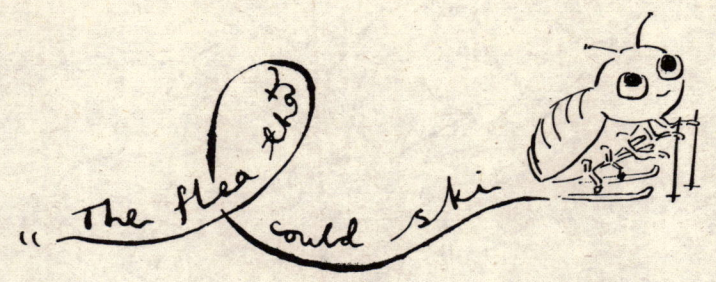

The flea that could ski
Went down a bowl full of sugar,
Only to discover
That it went faster on pasta.
Skiing on a baked bean made it scream,
In a Yorkshire pudding it could do a loop-de-loop
But then it all ended,
As it drowned quite happily
Attempting to water-ski in a bowl of soup.
The flea that could ski
Was easy to b u r y
In a flea cemetery.

Be careful with your words,
Once they are said
They can easily be misunderstood or misread.
Handle them with care,
Be careful not to drop them,
Sure, they can be forgiven
But never forgotten.
Words are free.
That's why we speak them easily
And sometimes so carelessly!
Yes, words are free it's true,
It's how you use them that may cost you.
Raise your words, not your voice.
It is rain that grows flowers, not thunder,
It's a whisper that makes everyone wonder.

One kind word can change someone's entire day,
So, think carefully about what you say.
Handle them carefully, for words have more power than you know.
They can make us small or make us grow.
With the magic to help and heal,
But they can hurt, harm, humiliate and humble.
Words can build an empire,
They can also make it crumble.
Kind words can be short and easy to speak,
But their echoes are truly endless and go deep.
Be careful what you say.
You can say something hurtful in ten seconds...
But ten years later, the wound still won't go away
Because words turn the world.
Don't underestimate the power of words.
Words move hearts,
Hearts move minds,
And minds can be cruel or kind.
Kind words are a creative force,
A message that can change history's course.
They are energy that showers blessings into each and everyone's life.
But the unkind ones cut like a knife.
Words do not fade
They cam be light as a feather or explode like a hand grenade.
Our words start wars, our words open doors
Our words can settle scores
Our words create our strengths
But also our weaknesses and flaws.
Before you open your mouth,
Make sure you carefully choose yours.

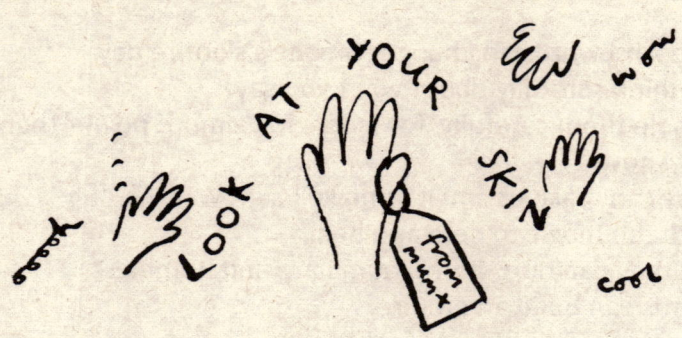

Look at your skin,
Yes, the one you are wearing.
Fits pretty good, as skin should,
That's because it was made by a mother's love.
Look at your skin,
Holding everything in.
Every bone, every dream and every feeling.
Every skin is the same,
Sometimes the colours change,
It might be Black it might be White
Or somewhere in between,
But every skin is exactly right,
And fits perfectly tight.
Now look at someone else's skin...
It looks and feels just like yours,
The colour might not be the same
It's a bit like eyes or hair
We also have different colours there.
But inside it's the same hopes and dreams we share.
There are so many names to describe the skin we wear.
Black, Brown, White, dark, pale, golden, bronzed,
caramel and fair.
But skin is something we all share.

So, the next time you see someone's skin,
Remember it's just like yours.
And that's why every skin deserves a round of applause.
So look at everyone's skin
Isn't it amazing,
Isn't it good?
And remember it's all the same,
Every skin is made out of a mother's love.

What do you SEE

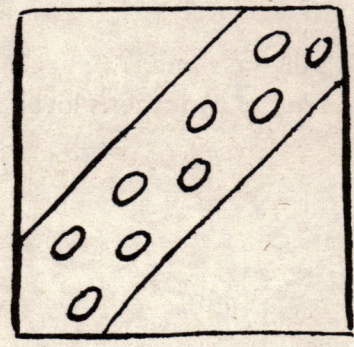

Is it a road filled with cars on the go?
Is it a river on which little boats flow?
Is it a scarf that's being stretched?
Is it the solution to some weird test?
Is it a parade of fried eggs?
Are they pillows to rest our heads?
Are they bubbles going up a straw?
Or is it seaweed washed up on the shore?
Is it a Brussel sprout sandwich?
Or are they the buttons on a lift?
Is it looking through a microscope?
Is it a display for a fancy shop selling soap?
Is it the tail of a kite?
Is it part of a bike?
Is it footprints on a path?
No, you are looking through a window
Being walked past by a giraffe!

The night we
made friends
with the

DARK

It was dark
It was night
Then out went the little
Bedroom light.
It wouldn't go back on,
The bulb had gone,
Only the moon shone
And we were left wondering...
About the shadows
Did the shadows have shadows?
While the only sound
Was the darkness all-around.
It was like being in space,
Or the world had become a different place
But where is the light?
It's in the stars, the headlamps of the passing cars.
The candle flames flickering
The luminescence of the clock face ticking.
The dark is like a kind of art
A world where we must be brave in our heart.
We must be brave whatever
Understand it together,
Because the dark will be here forever.

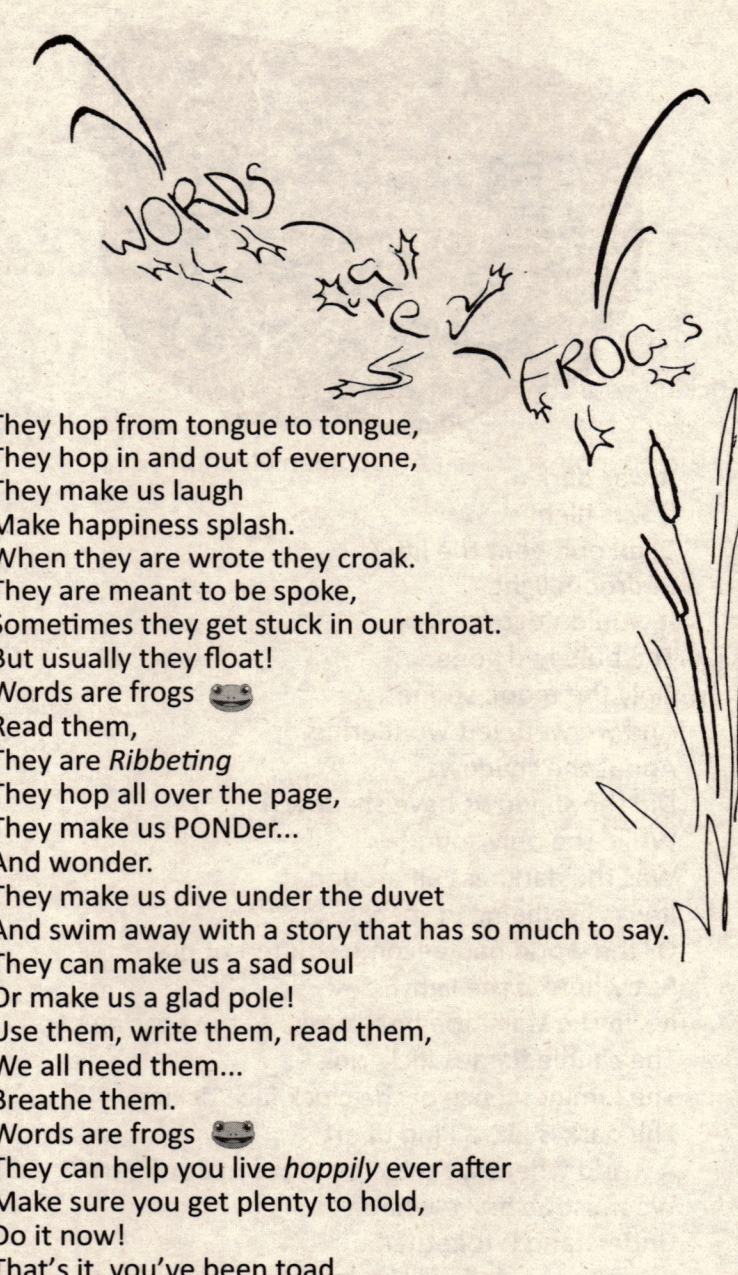

WORDS are FROGS

They hop from tongue to tongue,
They hop in and out of everyone,
They make us laugh
Make happiness splash.
When they are wrote they croak.
They are meant to be spoke,
Sometimes they get stuck in our throat.
But usually they float!
Words are frogs
Read them,
They are *Ribbeting*
They hop all over the page,
They make us PONDer...
And wonder.
They make us dive under the duvet
And swim away with a story that has so much to say.
They can make us a sad soul
Or make us a glad pole!
Use them, write them, read them,
We all need them...
Breathe them.
Words are frogs
They can help you live *hoppily* ever after
Make sure you get plenty to hold,
Do it now!
That's it, you've been toad.

TO BE CHEERFUL
-part me-

(dedicated to Ian Dury)

Sticking your tongue out at your reflection,
Making a sea-glass collection,
Getting people to vote for you in an election.

Trying to keep a snowflake alive,
Waiting for tomorrow to arrive,
Getting into bed with a dive.

Singing into the hairdryer,
Making a paper plane that's a flyer,
Getting wet then getting dryer.

Time travelling on the sofa,
Sitting in a cardboard box pretending you're a chauffeur,
Popping-up like a toaster.

Seeing a rainbow,
Helping to give birthday candles a blow,
Or just giving anything a go.

Making a baby laugh,
Making your own super hero mask,
Doing a fart in the bath.

Why don't you put a banana on your head,
Why don't you put a banana on your head,
Why don't you put a cuddly toy on your head,
Why don't you put a cushion on your head,
Why don't you put your mum on your head.

the benefits of food

Pasta makes you faster.
Broccoli makes you good at Monopoly.
Garlic makes you anarchic.
Porridge gives you knowledge.
Fish makes you good to kiss.
Cake helps you escape.
Custard makes you well adjusted.
Plantain makes you as strong as a mountain.
Soya will make you a good lawyer.
Crisps will help you take risks.
The skins of bananas
Can be sewn together to make good pyjamas.
Pizza will make you a teacher.
Oranges will give you lots of vitamin C
And keep you healthy.
What else do you think they'd be?

It's a book
Take a look
The pages never get stuck.

They turn
They burn
With poetic magic to learn.

There's word after word
Dying to be heard
Longing to be shared.

There's ideas
That make laughter and tears
Poems that shine like chandeliers.

There's lines
There's rhymes
Lyrical signs capturing good and bad times.

There's inspiration
From family and friends
There's illustration through the eye of a lens.

Yes, it's a book
The pages never get stuck
Always worth a look!

He could talk to turkeys
He could make words flow
Like the river Euphrates
He was a character as colourful as a box of Smarties
He could take you higher
He could fill you with poetic desire
He was Benjamin Zephaniah.

He could make you feel the light
He could make you hold the night
He could lyricise wrong and right
He could take you higher
He could fill you with poetic desire
He was Benjamin Zephaniah.

He wasn't once always that well-read or suited and
    booted
But this proud wearer of the dread achieved this with
    added street cred
And still remained deeply social rooted
He could take you higher
He could fill you with poetic desire
He was Benjamin Zephaniah.

He was stage, he was page
He was words ablaze
Always knew how to amaze
He was a social gauge!
When it came to the establishment
Boy could he rage... He was sage, he was fire
With the soul of a heavenly choir
He could take you higher
He could fill you with poetic desire
He was Benjamin Zephaniah.

fixing a yoyo

If your yo-yo's broken,
And it don't look good,
Who you gonna call –
Yo-yo busters!
No, cos' they only break them –
You are gonna call yo-yo fixers!
If the string won't spin
And your yo-yo won't do its thing,
Who you gonna call –
Yo-yo busters!
No, cos' they only break them –
You are gonna call yo-yo fixers!
If your yo-yo's tangled
And just can't be handled,
Who you gonna call –
Yo-yo busters!
No, cos they only break them –
You are gonna call yo-yo fixers!
I ain't afraid of no yo-yo,
I ain't afraid of no yo-yo,
I ain't afraid of no yo-yo,
I ain't afraid of no yo-yo,
Cos yo-yo'ing makes me feel good.
And fixing broken ones makes me feel even better.

A feather is clever
They withstand the weather
Help birds fly forever
Make beautiful patterns together.
A feather is a delight
In the olden days people used them to write.
They reflect the light
And keep you warm in a quilt at night.
A feather is an adventure
A gift from mother nature
A reminder of our tribal behaviour
A peacock's will amaze you.
Feathers, put them in your hair
Look after them, they are rare
And when you see birds flying
Feathers are the reason they are up there.

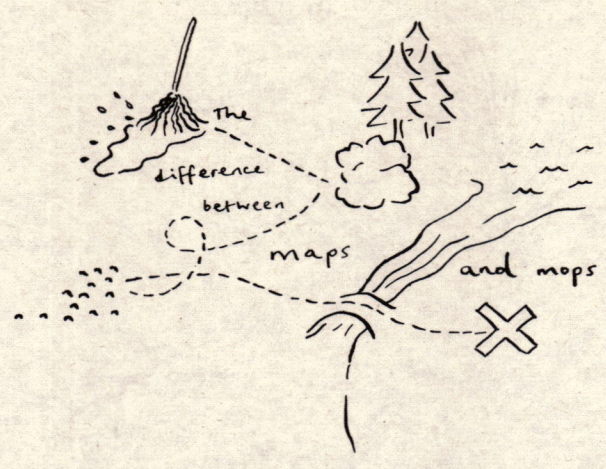

The difference between maps and mops

A map can show you where you've been,
A mop can show you where you've cleaned.
A map will take you places,
A mop will take you ages.
A map is an adventure waiting to begin,
A mop is an adventure in mopping.
A map can lead you to a secret door,
A mop can lead you to a dirty floor.
A map might have once been owned by a Roman or a
       Viking,
A mop probably belongs to someone a lot less exciting.
A map can be start of somewhere bewitching,
A mop can be the amazing beginning of a clean kitchen.

Maybe

Maybe MAYBE!

maybe

MAYBE!

Maybe

B

MAYBE

E

maybe

maybe

Maybe means yes,
Maybe means no,
Maybe means perhaps
But only if I say so.
Maybe means OK,
Maybe means no way,
Maybe means we will
But not necessarily today.
Maybe means if we must,
Maybe means eventually...
But only after it's been discussed!
Maybe means we still have the time,
Maybe means only if the sun does shine.
Maybe means maybe...
Maybe means don't be crazy
And maybe means stop acting like a baby.
Maybe this poem's finished and needs one last full stop.
Maybe means maybe it's not.
Maybe means soon,
Maybe means in the afternoon,
Maybe means right now,
Straight after you've cleaned up your room.

POM- BEARS

dedicated to
LYE Mikey

I had a packet of Pom-bears.
I put them on one of the chairs.
My friend sat on them.
My friend flattened them.
We opened up the bag of Pom,
The bears were all gone.
It was full of bits of legs, arms and ears,
The bears had disappeared.
Now it's just a bag of Pom.
The lesson is,
Be careful about what you sit on!

THE bUS

The bUS
Is for all of US
Takes US everywhere
Without any fUSs
Sometimes quick, sometimes slow
But it always takes US where we want to go.
The bUS...
Carries all of US
Sometimes to catch it we have to rUSh
Sometimes it's a bit of a crUSh
When the school kids get on there's not a lot of hUSh
But it will always be there for US
In that you can trUSt.
It can take you to AUStralia or the US of A
Though I think you have to change bUS
As there isn't one that goes all the way.
It's a plUS, it's a mUSt
BecaUSe the bUS
Is for all of US
(Feel free to discUSs)
PS when it comes to the bell don't repeatedly pUSh.

A is for angel,
B isn't!
C is for choosing the perfect Christmas
   present.
D is for didn't.
E is for Christmas Eve, when it's best to believe.
F is for Fanta, the favourite drink of Santa.
G is for gift,
H is for heavy, think about how many Santa has to lift.
I is for invasion, when all your family come round.
J is for festive jumpers that everyone wears around town.
K is for kissing under the mistletoe.
L is for love ❤ the star of the show.
M is for Mistletoe that's where Mary met Joe!
N is for the Nativity that brought hope to us.
O is for the Christmas Octopus.
P is for *paresents* that's a mixture of parents and
   presents.

Q is for queue, for parents taking presents back,

R is for receipt that they left back at their flat.

S is for socks and that's what you get when you don't
believe in Santa.

T is for tinsel - don't get it in a tangle.

U is for universal love.

V is for *Vixen & Comet & Donner & Blitzen*
Dancer & Prancer who pull Santa's sleigh with all their
might,

No I've not forgotten Rudolph but he's just more of a
headlight.

W is wrapping paper that has been ripped to bits.

X is for Xmas for making possible this list.

Y is for yelling happy Christmas...

To all of those who need us, feed us and believe in us.

Z is for the reason it exists, little baby *Zesus.*

Butterflies are paintings in disguise
Sent to dazzle our eyes.
Their beautiful wings are painted so delicately,
They are art galleries of fragility.
They lift us above.
Their wings are shaped like two heart-joined-together
    symbols of love.
They begin life as a caterpillar,
They transform to have beautiful wings that are their
    superpower.
A gift of nature,
We decorate our world with their picture.
They don't last long,
They are here then gone,
But every summer they come
Flutter by, flutter on.

Boy Band POEM 4EVA

Baby, baby, baby, baby, baby, baby,
Baby, baby, baby, baby, baby, baby,
Baby, baby, baby, baby, baby, baby,
Our love can't be wrong, now go out,
And buy this song.

Girl Band POEM xoxo xoxo

Honey, honey, honey, honey, honey,
Honey, honey, honey, honey, honey,
Honey, honey, honey, honey, honey,
Even though we can't sing,
Your love means everything.

THE SHARK THAT LIVED IN A TREE

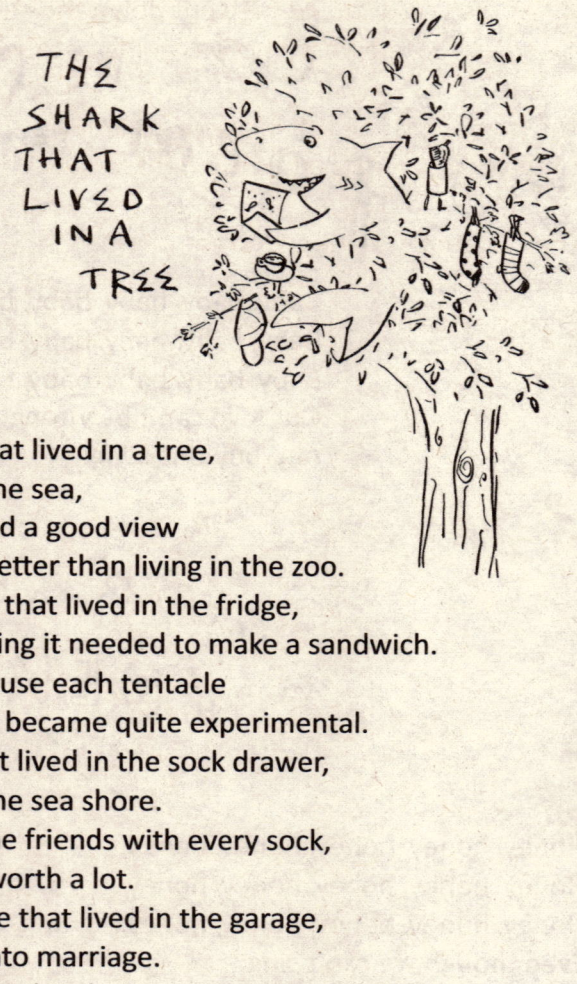

The shark that lived in a tree,
Never saw the sea,
But it still had a good view
And it was better than living in the zoo.
The octopus that lived in the fridge,
Had everything it needed to make a sandwich.
It still got to use each tentacle
And actually became quite experimental.
The crab that lived in the sock drawer,
Never saw the sea shore.
But it became friends with every sock,
And that is worth a lot.
The crocodile that lived in the garage,
Was really into marriage.
It didn't like to be alone
And hoped one day to be Mr & Mrs Croc and move into a
    home.
The panda that lived in a military tank,
Didn't know who to thank.

He would crush cars as he went down the street,
He never looked where he was going because he was
   asleep.
The penguin that lived in an ice cream van,
Simply said everyone has the right to live wherever they
   can.
The penguin gave out ice cream for free,
How do I know?
Because he gave one to me.

AWAKE TO A KISS

Once upon a time
In the beginning of my mind,
Fair princesses more lovely than the dawn,
Roamed the earth with 'tough on tangle hair'.
Or were awakened from their dreaming,
By princes with boy-band looks
And smiles that were beaming,
Who would declare – 'your garden has got quite
Out of hand and your stepmother is difficult
And bewildering -
Between you and me
I think she eats children,
On all fours, even yours.'
Charmed by these words and the stolen
Way they were spoken,
Grateful that the evil magic was broken,
She fell madly in love as one does.
'My heart is yours, please unlock it.
You can carry my glass coffin,
So long as you promise not to drop it.'

Now, princes may be handsome and kind
But they only have marriage and child-bearing on
   their mind.
While the only thing about a princess's appearance
   that's wrong,
Is it's all she's judged on.
So, as you are happy, so be wise.
Fairy tales are reality in disguise...
And this you'll find,
Is how it exactly happened,
Except it didn't rhyme.

They say less is more,
Unless we are talking about cake.

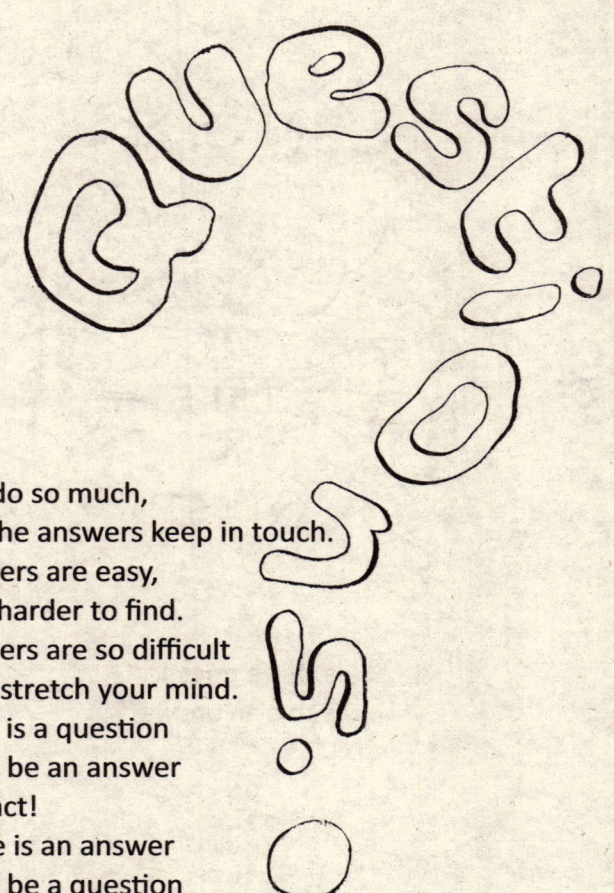

Questions do so much,
They help the answers keep in touch.
Some answers are easy,
Others are harder to find.
Some answers are so difficult
They really stretch your mind.
But if there is a question
There must be an answer
– that's a fact!
And if there is an answer
There must be a question
Waiting to be asked.

Is this a question?
Is this an answer?

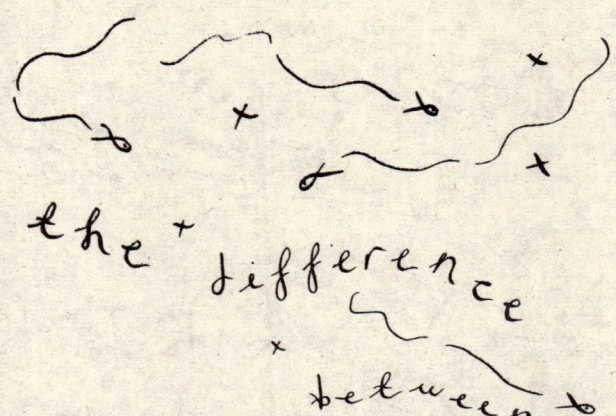

the difference between fishes and kisses

Kisses, are just a cross.
Fishes, are a cross
With a curve
And an eye that's a dot -
They also swim about a lot.

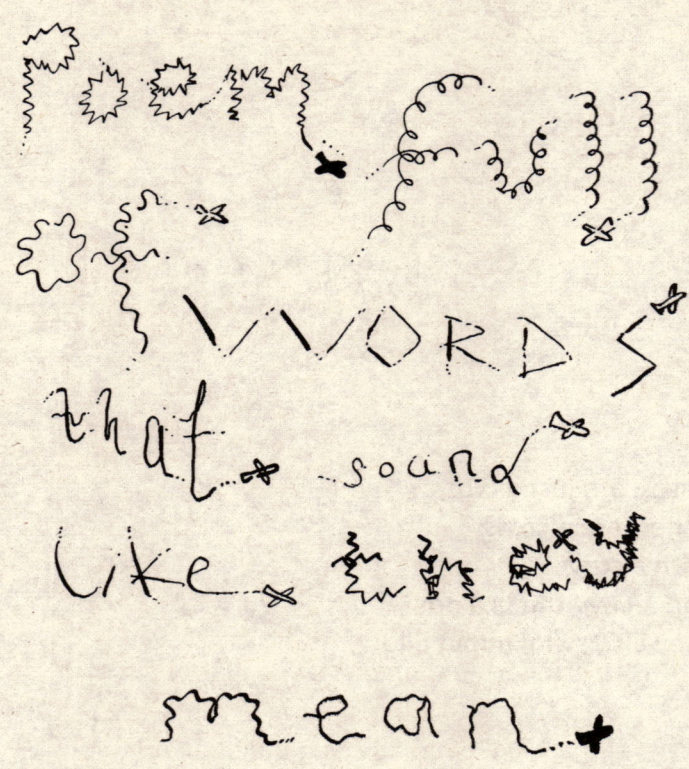

Poem full of words that sound like they mean

Scribbling – squiggling – wiggling – giggling
Gurgling – burbling – gibbering – dribbling
Babbling – squabbling – bobbling – wobbling
Waggling –
Heathrow Airport Terminal Four

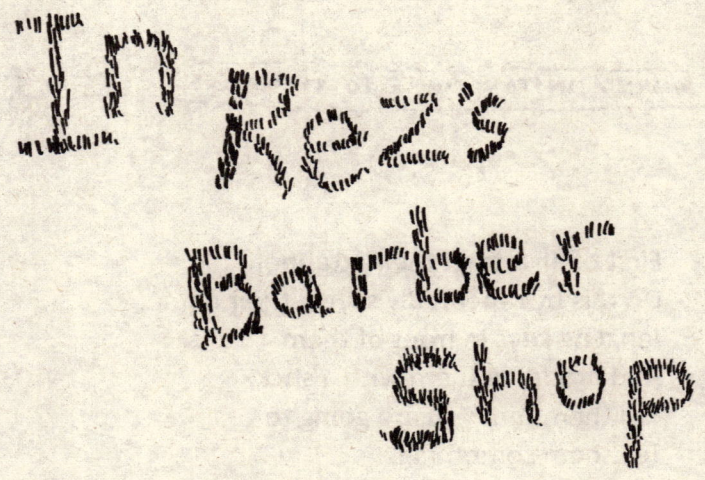

In Rez's Barber Shop

A man walked into Rez's Barber Shop
and sat in one of the barbers chairs.
Took off his hat and said,
'Who wants to see a million hairs!'

GIVING INSTRUCTIONS TO TEENAGES

First of all attract their attention.
Do this by repeatedly saying their name,
Jangling keys in front of them
And prodding them with a stick.
Tell them that you are going to
Tell them something.
At this point, jangle the keys again
And prod them some more with the stick.
If you are sending them to the shop
For a loaf of bread,
Show them what a loaf of bread looks like.
This will stop them becoming confused
And coming back with something totally different,
Like a cabbage, or a toilet seat.
Don't forget to write down their name
And address, and tie it to their arm.
Repeat the instructions one more time,
Prod them with the stick some more.
By now, this will not make them remember
The instructions any better
But it is good fun.

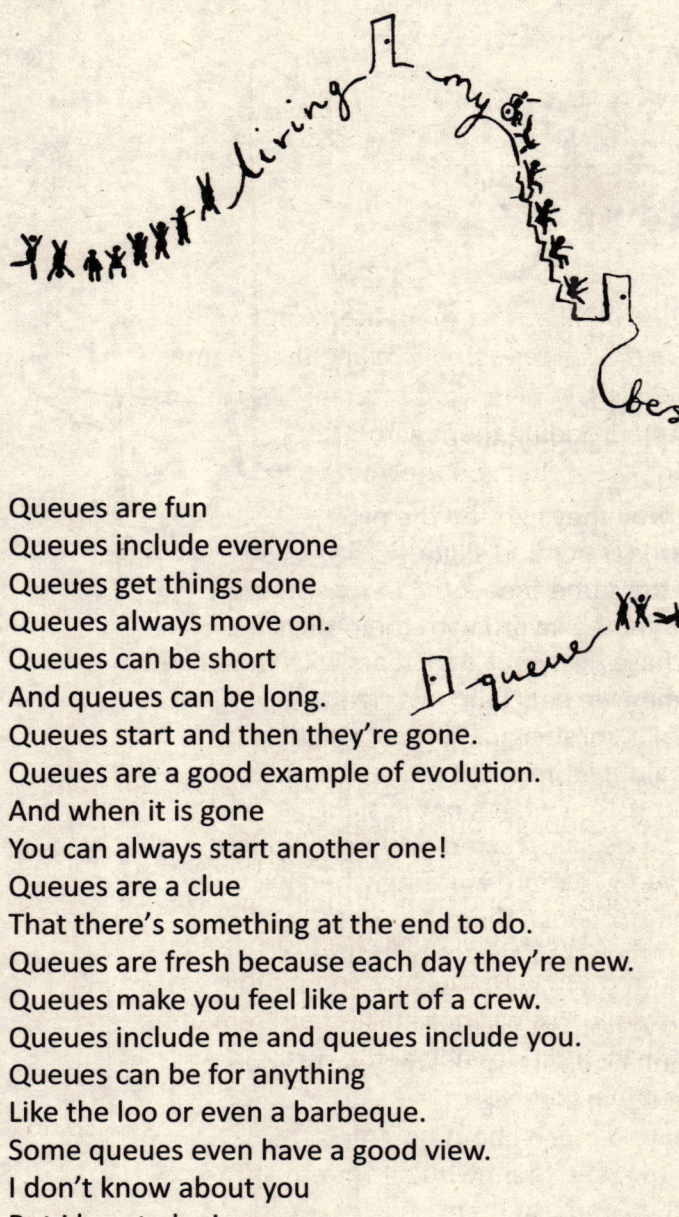

living my

best

queue

Queues are fun
Queues include everyone
Queues get things done
Queues always move on.
Queues can be short
And queues can be long.
Queues start and then they're gone.
Queues are a good example of evolution.
And when it is gone
You can always start another one!
Queues are a clue
That there's something at the end to do.
Queues are fresh because each day they're new.
Queues make you feel like part of a crew.
Queues include me and queues include you.
Queues can be for anything
Like the loo or even a barbeque.
Some queues even have a good view.
I don't know about you
But I love to be in a queue.

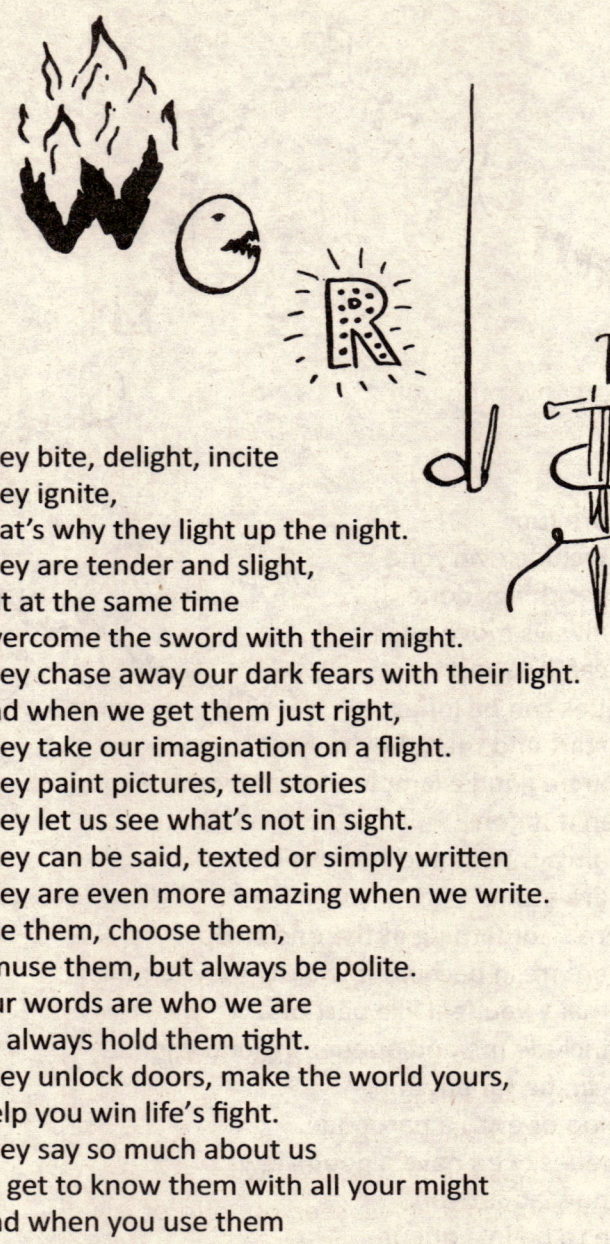

They bite, delight, incite
They ignite,
That's why they light up the night.
They are tender and slight,
But at the same time
Overcome the sword with their might.
They chase away our dark fears with their light.
And when we get them just right,
They take our imagination on a flight.
They paint pictures, tell stories
They let us see what's not in sight.
They can be said, texted or simply written
They are even more amazing when we write.
Use them, choose them,
Amuse them, but always be polite.
Our words are who we are
So always hold them tight.
They unlock doors, make the world yours,
Help you win life's fight.
They say so much about us
So get to know them with all your might
And when you use them
Make sure you get them just right.

It's great being a DAD

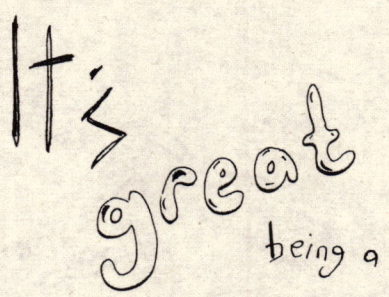

'Were you down the pub,
Watching Leeds thrash Manchester City
5-2 on a giant TV screen?
Some people say it was the
Best FA cup tie ever seen!'
'No, I was with my kid,
Making a model of the rainforest
From a shoe box lid,
Plasticine, cocktail sticks,
Silver foil for a river and a stream,
Toilet paper which we had to paint green!
Little plastic animals here there and in-between.'
'But this was the greatest FA cup-tie -
EVER SEEN!
End to end scoring shots against the bar,
The crowd non-stop roaring, every player a star.
Shots against the post,
It was all about who would score the most.
Football not to be missed,
Football that had every twist,
Football that was the best of the best...'
'Yeah, well you should have seen our rainforest.'

Spider catcher
Sofa relaxer
Sandwich manufacturer
Baby distracter
Dad-dancing disaster
Bed-time-story-book happily ever after!
Endless supply of laughter
Shower singing X-Factor
World Cup football master
Another Dad joke coming at yer',
Shoulder taxi for tired kids who have become a collapser
Lego building subcontractor
Hard working grafter
Romantic as a tractor
Bad actor
Arse scratcher.

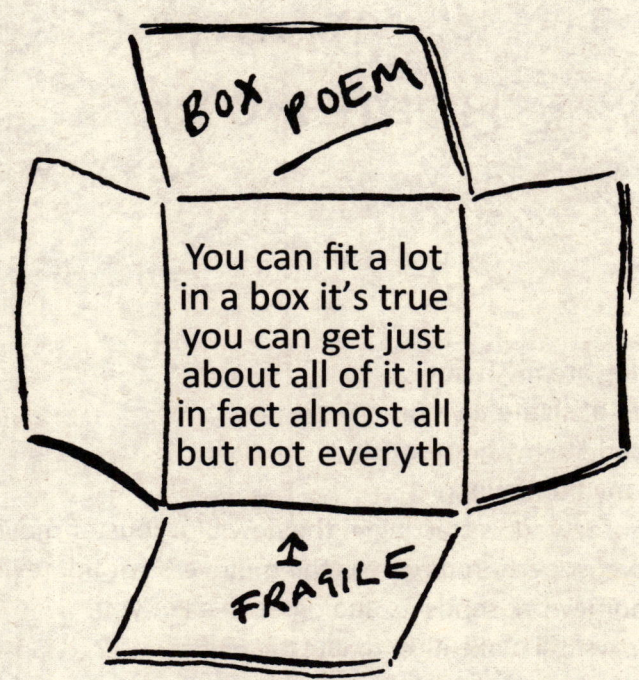

Excuses for not Doing your HOMEWORK

My dog ate my homework.
My goldfish ate my homework.
My dad ate my homework.
I ate my homework.
My homework is starring in the new blockbuster movie
'Marvel superheroes versus the multiverse of homework'.
My homework sends its apologies to all of you,
And says it'll make it up to later
By taking everyone to the zoo.
My homework is being haunted by a ghost.
My homework's looking after my poorly little sister.
My homework is out there fighting crime.
My homework is taking part in
Strictly Come Homework
And needs to learn the Argentinian Tango by Saturday.

It's also on...
I'm Homework Get Me Out Of Here.
Homework Patrol (always on the double)
The Great British Homework Bake Off
And Britain's Got Homework Talent!
My homework fell in love with some other homework
And they are doing something ro-man-tic ❤!
Look, it's not coming in,
Just accept it!

Saturday morning ballet class

Ballerinas dressed in blue,
Unable to stand still, always twisting,
    turning,
Doing something new.
Swaying from toe to toe,
Caught in a show of movement and flow.
A blue chain that sways again and again,
Moves like a flame,
Unsure across the wooden floor,
Making the same mistakes as before –
Making beautiful shapes that fully explore
The awe of movement, that sings,
To the sound of the piano key's rings.
Little limbs trying to do grown-up things,
Trying to fly with tiny wings.
Ballerinas dressed in blue,
Unable to stand still.
Spinning, twisting, turning, doing something new.
Trying to do what the 'ballet teacher tells you'.
But little ballerinas dressed in blue
Dance only as they do.

for Honor and Suria

My daughters, don't always do the things
They ought'a.
They like a bath, but only if there's
Hot water.
They're getting taller,
Not shorter.
When they found me going through their secret
    sweets-stash
They said, 'Caught yer!'
When they sing, 'Go greased lightning, you're
burning through the quarter mile,'
It's exactly in the style
of John Travolta.
When their noses are blocked,
They become a bit of a snorter.
And when they grow up,
I hope that each of them,
Remember
All the things that love
has taught her.

London Town going round,
Never free from sound.
Red buses rumble,
Riding through a concrete jungle.
People sliding down busy streets,
London Town never sleeps
- this city's got a fast heartbeat.
Somewhere to go, someone to meet.
The car-jam's beeps,
Even the night-time leaps,
With flashing lights, sound bites,
Rain-soaked streets
Above tube train seats,
Below aeroplane flights.
Rainbow neon lights
FLASH,
- reflecting in shop window glass.
A thousand faces go past,
London Town goes on, goes fast.
There's a shop for everyone,
And everything,
'Come on in'.

London Town built around
A human race meltdown.
Four corners of the earth
Sharing their worth.
Look around there's always
Someone to be found
In London Town.

it's great to illustrate

for Lizzie C and Joseph W

Way back when,
The cave women and men
Began it all by illustrating...
Their lives, their tribe,
The animals they lived with,
Hunters who were hunted, trying to survive.
They drew round their hand,
Left a finger portrait for us to understand.
Back then they did it on the walls of a cave,
But that's because they were Stone Age.
Nowadays it's much easier you can do it on a page,
Your imagination is the stage.
Sketch or draw what you see or saw,
Mix ink, felt tip or paint together there isn't any law.
Set the characters and creatures inside you free
Capture faces and places for everyone to see,
Mix in a bit of graffiti and calligraphy.
Shape, define and blend and bend minds
And yes it's ok to colour outside of the lines.
Just doodle, you don't need approval.
Just like the great Joseph Witchall,

Pickle and pallete the pixel
Or like the gifted Lizzie Clark
Take your talent and make it spark.
So grab your creativity,
Set it free,
Remove it from its cage
Don't keep your art or heart hidden in a cave.
We are all artists from birth
And without art there is no eARTh.

Swimming in a shining sea of life

Dolphins are really clever.
They can tell where they are
By looking at the stars.
Or know how near to land,
By sending noise waves
That echo rocks and sand.
They like to dance and frolic,
And make their own music.
When they leap clear of the waves
They see a cluster of birds dining on fish
And they're there too, in a tail's swish.
They can also make a milkshake
Play the drums, fly a kite,
Ride a bike and are good at wiggling their bums.
On Saturday afternoons
They like to make TikTok films and wear
T-shirts that say,
'Don't judge this fish because I'm wearing
A T-shirt with a message written on it' !
When dolphins say, 'Hello'
They do it by saying, 'Gimme' 5' or 'What's up'!
Sometimes, dolphins graffiti boats.
The thing they like to write the most -
'SEE YOU - WOULDN'T WANT TO BE YOU.'

Are we there yet?
Not quite.
Where are we then?
We're nearly there.
Where's nearly there?
It's near to here.
Where's here?
Somewhere.
Somewhere's everywhere!
We're there, or there-abouts.
There's no such place!
There is!
Where's it near?
It's near to there.
Not there?
No, near to nearly there.
I wish we were anywhere!
That's in the other direction!
Are we almost nearly there yet?
Not quite.
Where exactly are we?
We're between nearly there and almost there.
Oh, now I know where we are.

We need courage,
Like a sofa needs a bottom
And a good memory needs not to be forgotten.
We need dreams,
Like Aladdin needs Jasmine
And a question needs answering.
We need respect,
Like a tiger needs stripes
And a YouTuber needs likes.
We need love,
Like a bubble bath needs bubbles
And a baby needs cuddles.
We need peace,
Like feet need socks
And a Star Trek party needs lots of Mr Spocks!
We need friendship,
Like football needs a referee
And every argument needs two people to disagree.
We need family,
Like the alphabet needs every letter
And someone who is sad needs someone to make them
   feel better.

Alternative uses for rainbows

Funky eyebrows on funky eyebrow day.
Hats to keep the rain away.
Handles on suitcases,
Sky rides to take you places.
Shoe laces or extremely bright mazes.
Classroom seats!
Pavements in extremely colourful streets.
Cots for babies,
Earings for ladies.
Two together to make a colourful tyre,
Plug one in and you've got a cosmic hairdryer.
Put them over rivers as bridges,
Doors for fridges.
Bathroom showers that wash you with colour without
    any itches.
Goal posts for football pitches
The ends of broomsticks for fashionable witches.
Let's not forget what they do best
Show that rain and sun mixed together makes us all
    blessed.

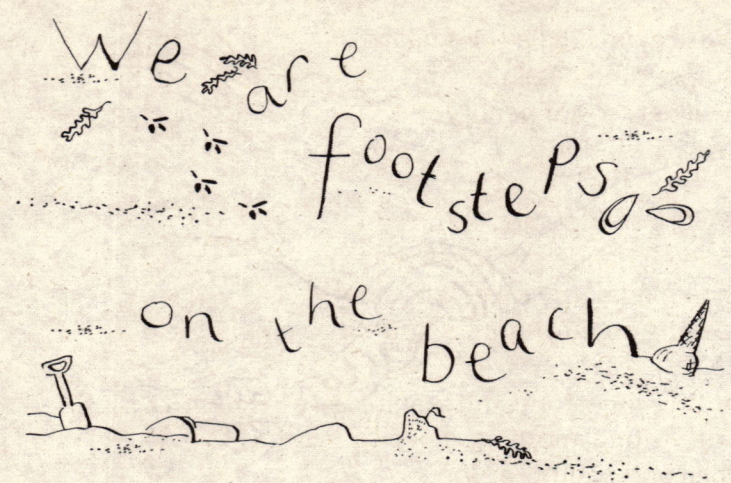

We are footsteps on the beach

We are the rear-view mirror housing estate
The great break of the epic landscape
Who's going to see the sea first
Back-seat VIPs so excited they'll burst.

We are sandcastles in the rain
The kids want the toilet again!
Sandwiches with a hint of sand
And other ingredients MasterChef wouldn't understand.

We are in awe as dolphins break the surface
We've got free front row seats for their water circus
Sea birds performing unique acrobatics
It's the ultimate aeronautical aquatics.

We are Jurassic Lego, block upon block
Pieced together by the land time forgot
We are pirate, mermaid, smuggler and Attenborough
Mixed with pyrite, lemonade, juggler and burrower.

We are drawing a sand heart
Where time began to start
A wilderness of beauty
We are off duty.

We are sandcastles in the sun
Holding hands with someone
Riding on our families' shoulders
Making memories for when we're older.

We are limestone and granite
Like visiting another planet
Shell and beautiful stone
Choosing which ones to take home.

We are the coast
The day we loved the most
Where the sea meets the sky
Where the land says goodbye.

We are an early morning like no other
Seaweed that stretches like rubber!
A cotton towel island on a sea of sand
Checking every five minutes to see if we're getting tanned.

We are the cry of the seabird
We are a white horse breaker herd
We are soft dunes, fragility and imposing cliffs
We are all of this.

We are sand between the toes
Winding paths that go where no-one knows
A first kiss
A salty silent nothingness...

Why are you still in bed?
Wake up.
Get up.
No.
Stop.
Ssshhh.
Hush.
If you must!
Listen.
Did I give you permission?
Stop talking.
Start walking.
Get a move on.
Faster.
No you can't have a plaster!

Now.
How?
No way!
Back in my day...
What did I just say?
Finish what's on your plate.
We're going to be late.
Sit up straight.
Did you hear what I said?
Bed!

A shopping list for a creative childhood

Conkers, imagination, conkers, freedom, conkers, risks,
 and more conkers.
A limitless universe, going forward in reverse,
Full of big Wonder, big Imagination, big Opportunities
 and big conkers!
Free to play, associate, make friends and the odd mistake.
Free to take a risk, free to stick or twist,
Free to pick and choose
The conkers that are good for you.
Each child is an individual,
As individual as Willy Wonka!
As unique as each conker.
Wild diversity in the University of the Child,
Free to let your conker twirl,
Making your own world out of confidence and experience,
Resilient and truthful,
Messy and beautiful –
Sometimes a beautiful mess,
But it's not a test.

Eyes wide, eyes shut
To unlock the colours of your imagination,
Especially if that colour is chestnut!
Dancing like nobody's watching, throwing a ball with
nobody catching.
It's meeting, embracing, speaking – it's all these things,
It's conkers with strings!
It's within reach, it's conkers on a beach!
Scribbling and dancing, it's your past and future getting
    together and romancing.
A daydream of being accepted, it's a conker being
    inspected.
A smile, a place, a space, to be free, to be me,
It's getting conkers out of a tree,
It's watching them fall,
Yes, a creative childhood conquers all.

This is the start of the end,
The beginning of the last page.
Everything has a beginning and an end.
About half way through there's a middle bit.
We haven't reached it yet.
We are now pretty much at the end of the beginning of
    the start of the last poem.
As promised here comes the middle bit.
It's neither a start or an end,
But even the middle bit has a start and also a finish.
Middle bits are a bit like being on plane in flight,
Floating through the clouds...
Between countries in an endless blue.

Unlike the start and end of plane journeys,
All bumps and screaming engines,
The ground rushing around just outside the window.
That's the end of the middle bit,
Now it's time for the beginning of the end bit.
The plane landing if you like.
Have we learned anything from this poem?
Well da, yes,
Every new beginning comes from some other beginning's
    end.
We've also learned that words, are like frogs,
They can hop about,
Be hard to hold, or magically retold.
And if you kiss them just right,
Words and frogs that is,
They can be turned into something beautiful -
A fun-to-be-with wonderful!
Right here's the end (as promised)
Thank you for flying Paul Lyalls Poetry Airways.
We hope you enjoy your never ending reading holiday.
Every book is a hotel,
Every page is a day out.
Sorry, it was supposed to be ending.
Don't get me started!

Paul Lyalls - Poet in residence for the ROALD DAHL Museum 2013/2014 & Star of BBC2's/CBBC's 'Big Slam poetry House'. His poetry is funny and moving and his poetry workshops produce extraordinary poems from children of all ages. Paul has been poet in residence at 14 Secondary Schools and 21 Primary Schools. Paul was Poet for the London Borough of Brent (London's 5th coolest Borough) and he performed at the new Wembley Stadium. He has 2 poems in Michael Rosen's 'The A-Z of the best Children's Poetry'. Paul has also performed at 10 Edinburgh festivals, 1 Eton College, 5 Glastonbury's and on a 73 Bus, which made the and finally...bit of the 6pm national news. Paul has worked & performed with Michael Rosen, George Best, Miranda Hart, Kae Tempest, John Hegley, Benjamin Zepphaniah, John Cooper Clark & Rastamouse to name but a few. Paul was a London 2012 Olympic 'Shake the Dust' Poet & 2012 Smile London Poet. Paul has regularly worked with Arsenal Football club (Yes that one) performing his poetry in their dressing room and on their pitch!

'Paul is a kind of magic that makes you see the world in a different way' - Michael Rosen

'With 100 Year 5 children, you certainly inspired and injected enthusiasm both for the children & the staff...you allowed quirky and fun moments of their lives to be captured and it was something that children of all abilities could connect and spark from. we all loved re-reading our poems.'
                    Head of year Danes Hill School.

'Thank you again for your amazing session with Year 4. Not only did they love it but I did too! So many helpful tips on how to introduce and teach poetry.
                    'Literacy Lead, William Tyndale Primary School.

www.paul-lyalls.co.uk

Acknowledgments:

Special thanks to all at Authors Abroad / Caboodle books
(for being so great) - and if you would like to book me to visit
your school please contact the team at:
general@caboodlebooks.co.uk

And also to my amazing creative team - to Joseph Witchall
(cover design), Lizzie Clark (page illustrations)
and Angela Lawless (typesetting and formatting).

Also available from Paul Lyalls:

A Funny Thing Happened!